A Vermonter's Heritage:

LISTENING TO THE TREES

Poems by
RICK BESSETTE

Rick Bessette

Published by Wind Ridge Books
P.O. Box 595
Shelburne, Vermont 05482
www.windridgebooks.org

ISBN Number 978-1-935922-00-1

Design by Margo Callaghan
Printed in Burlington, Vt. U.S.A.

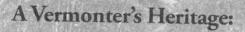

A Vermonter's Heritage:

LISTENING
TO THE
TREES

Poems by
RICK BESSETTE

Published by Wind Ridge Books
Shelburne, Vermont

"Seek peace and pursue it."

Psalm 34, Verse 14

About the Poet

*R*ick Bessette says, "I'm a hound dog loose on the farm." And if you think about that statement, you know a lot about Rick. He's constantly on the search for the beauty, the sights, the scents, the images of the spectacular and historic place where he has lived his entire life: Shelburne Farms. The Farm has given him a very personal experience of nature and he knows the peace and harmony that nature can have on the human soul. His poetry reflects his observations of people, wildlife, and the abundant woodlands and mountain vistas of Vermont. And that "hound dog" remark speaks to the sense of humor that leavens his words.

Rick loves to share his poetic observations of nature, the changing seasons, and the mysteries of life with others.

In addition to poetry, Rick is also an accomplished woodcarver. His duck decoys are on display in nine states and three countries.

Rick and his wife Candy live in Shelburne Village and he continues to work on and around Shelburne Farms, as do their two sons, Jeremy and Travis.

-Rosalyn Graham
Director of Community and Public Relations for Shelburne Farms

Author's Note

*M*y father worked and lived on Shelburne Farms for most of his life. I have also lived there and spent my entire working life managing properties on the estate. My two sons were raised on the Farm and now they work there too. Three generations of my family have been connected to Shelburne Farms.

I also had four uncles that worked on the Farm in its early years. One of those uncles, Joe Thomas, also wrote rhyming quatrains; the impulse to write everyday poems about life and the beauty of Vermont's landscape seems to run in the family.

Initially, I only wrote poems occasionally; however, after both a falling accident that required months of bed rest and the death of my father, I began to take more notice of the beauty and the peace in the things that I see and hear every day. And I began to take note and to write more frequently.

I no longer live on the Farm, but live nearby and work still brings me there almost every day. I also no longer take "simple" things for granted and try to capture these moments in words. It is a very rich heritage and one for which I am truly grateful.

CONTENTS

CHAPTER 3
Trees and Flowers

CHAPTER 4
Land and Lake

Dedication

To my wife Candy and my two sons, Jeremy and Travis

CHAPTER 1

From the Heart

Can I Touch
Your Heart

*L*isten to these words
As if leaves softly fall,
Let thoughts slowly drift;
Peace, it won't hurt at all.

I'll paint restful pictures
Somewhere far away,
Far from useless clutter
Crowding every day.

Can I touch your heart
With simple words I write?
Add joy to the day
And peace unto the night.

Uncle Joe

I laid my warm hand gently
Upon the cool granite stone,
And looked around to make sure
That I stood quite alone.

A moment left for silence
To respect his resting place,
Then recalled his funny laugh
His round and smiling face.

I still have all his stories
Written in poetic rhyme,
Each one I'll always cherish
The rest of my lifetime.

The reason I came and spoke,
I wanted to let you know,
When I write my rhyming verse
I think of Uncle Joe.

*This poem was written to pay homage
to my Uncle Joe Thomas who wrote
poetry more than 40 years ago; his
handwritten collection of poems was
his legacy to me and has influenced my
quatrain style of writing poetry.*

Dove of Peace

Pure is its color
And soft is its sound,
Living in harmony
Where gentleness is found.

Time is its witness,
To love it has brought
Keys to our universe
That so many have sought.

It's my wish for you,
Find peace all year long;
May your heart be opened
By tranquility's song.

*I sent this poem as a Christmas
card in 2008 to former President
George W. Bush at the White
House and to Vermont's
Senator Patrick Leahy and was
acknowledged and thanked by both.*

Reward

The most rewarding feeling
In writing poetry I'd say,
Is to touch a person's heart
Where all the true emotions lay.

It's not becoming published
Or the prize money you can win,
It's that this heartfelt writing
Releases feelings from within.

If there's truth in what you write
About living out each day,
The lessons noted then are shared,
When we triumph or we stray.

When a heartfelt note or call
Comes to this lone author who wrote,
It stirs again strong feelings,
Raising a lump right in my throat.

Evening Shadows

Shadows on the ceiling
From a candle flame now low,
Its small fire dances softly
And leaves a gentle glow.

Evening has cast her spell,
A long day now put to rest,
As you climb into your bed
Like songbirds in their nest.

The mind begins to drift
As you send your thanks above,
Peace settles the restless heart
That took the time to love.

Remember the
Good Things

*O*n the darkest of days
When the heart hurts deep,
When nights become long,
And you toss in your sleep -

Remember the good things
That life brought your way:
The bright starry nights
And the warm summer days,

The rainbows and sunsets
That color the sky,
Arrival of spring
When the songbirds stop by.

Footprints on
my Heart

Our footprints left behind
On summer's sandy beach,
All heaven's stars that night
Just barely out of reach.

Only to fade in time
Washed by the endless sea,
The tiny grains of sand
That carried you and me.

With your soft hand in mine,
'Twas that of priceless art,
For on that star-filled night
You left footprints on my heart.

The Little Things

It's the little things in life
That makes it so worthwhile,
Tender things that touch your heart,
Small things that make you smile.

The scent of fresh-brewed coffee,
The light at early dawn,
Watching red robins in spring
Worm hunting on the lawn;

Light shining on calm waters
Presented by the moon,
An echo off the shoreline
Sung by a lonesome loon;

Laughter, stories, and campfire,
Marshmallows on a stick,
A candle's soft magic glow
Brought by the burning wick;

It's the quiet that is found
Beside a mountain stream,
Where nature provides a place
For us to come and dream.

Letting Go

Somewhere from the other side
Of mountains dressed for fall,
The morning sun crept aloft
To give a wake-up call.

Waited just outside your door
To greet you with hello,
Tried to lay my sorrow down
Because you had to go.

But in my heart I'll carry
Fond memories that we made,
Underneath your apple trees
Enjoying their cool shade.

We shared the view looking west,
Great beauty for our eyes,
Spoke of pleasure in the taste
Of homemade apple pies.

It's so hard to say goodbye,
But yes...it must be so;
This sad farewell breaks my heart
The final letting go.

This poem was written about
a friend on the day he passed away.

Where Fallen Heroes Go

*Y*ou've left behind some memories
That time can't wash away.
You've gone on to a higher place
Where fallen heroes play.

Our hearts are completely broken,
Smiles are not the same,
Our voices do still speak aloud
In honor of your name.

Your picture sits on the mantle
With letters writ by hand,
All the medals that you had earned
Now framed on our nightstand.

We know somewhere up in the clouds
Beyond the need of wings,
Forevermore your days are spent
With angels, saints, and kings.

*Written in memory of SPC Scott McLaughlin who
was killed in action in Iraq on September 22, 2005.*

Time Spent
With Frost

I came to visit
You were not there,
But through weathered glass
I saw your chair.

Out on the green lawn
Maples stood guard,
With old tired limbs
Shading the yard.

The old fieldstone wall
Your hands once built,
Stills stands in its place
But tends to tilt.

I will always wish
Our paths had crossed;
I'd shake the great hand
Of Robert Frost.

*This poem was written after
a visit to Robert Frost's home
in Ripton, Vermont.*

The Puddle

*H*ave you ever stopped to look
In a puddle on the ground?
If the water's clear enough,
Your reflection might be found.

Contented with whom you see
Looking clearly back at you?
Are you proud or embarrassed
With all the things that you do?

Someone is always watching –
Good examples need be set.
Be careful near that puddle,
'Cause your face may end up wet.

So, if you can see yourself
And smile, then go on your way.
Give thanks for all your blessings,
And for what reflections say.

CHAPTER 2

Looking to the Skies

Sunrise

I sat upon the grassy knoll
Still wet with heavy dew,
Watched the new morning haze give way
And sun come into view.

Shedding light on the Green Mountains
And valleys far below,
Silent sunrays reveal once more
The place I've come to know.

Waiting there just a little while,
Pondering what it's worth,
Sitting on the grassy knoll
It's the richest place on earth.

Breakfast
With Butterflies

We sat there together
Under shade of tall trees,
Enjoying our breakfast
And were kissed by the breeze.

When two butterflies came
From the still morning sky,
Our eyes followed their flight
On their way passing by.

They circled our table
In the cool mountain air,
With their delicate wings
And great beauty to share.

When breakfast was finished
And our time there was through,
They left on their journey
In skies cloudless and blue.

Sounds in the Night

A walk after dark
In woods of white pine,
I'm holding your hand
And you're holding mine.

The only sounds heard
While walking the road,
Were crickets and frogs
And little tree toads.

The moon's crescent light
And nature's sounds too,
Were stirring my heart
While walking with you.

S'mores Night

*T*he weather's looking good
And Fridays almost here,
The fire pit is loaded
Lawn chairs are circled near.

Chocolate and marshmallows
Graham crackers by the box,
The workweek now has ended
No need for pesky clocks.

Friends and family gather
The neighbors show up too
S'mores night in the backyard
The stars provide the view.

This is how we like to spend a Friday
evening after a busy workweek; our
neighbors introduced us to the pleasures
of this weekly event.

January Thaw

*T*he sun's misplaced
It seems today,
Instead, there's rain:
Cold, damp, and grey.

Away with snow
That had been deep,
A winter's dream
Kids hoped to keep.

But things will change
Again we know,
Winter's cold winds
Will bring more snow.

Rising Moon

I watched you rise
One summer night
A round golden glow
And glorious sight.

You took your place
Among the stars
Keeping company
With Venus and Mars.

Just out of reach
You seem to be
Suspended aloft
In heaven's great sea.

Evening Show

Raspberry swirls
In summer's warm sky,
Left by a sunset
To please our eye.

As evening falls
Swirls fade out of sight,
A full moon rises
Lighting the night.

If

*I*f I could ride the morning sun
Across the clear blue sky,
Or spread my wings like the songbirds
And destinations fly;

If I could climb up a rainbow
Slide down the other side,
Or speak the language of the stars,
To them, I would confide.

If I could sit among the clouds
Play games of hide and seek,
And listen as do the angels,
Then I would hear God speak.

First Snow

*E*ven the moon and stars
Couldn't stir the heart this way,
When winter's first fall of snow
Landed on the trees to stay.

Brought by a cold north wind,
Snow hung on the windowsill.
All had gone to sleep by now,
The world fell silent and still.

Mixed with the dark of night
Were tiny white flakes that fell,
A gift from Mother Nature
When she cast a peaceful spell.

Evening Magic

It rose in slow motion
Above snow-covered ground –
How can something so big
Arrive without sound?

In clarity it grew,
Well beyond mortal's reach
Needs no introduction
And no endless speech.

Casts a soft glowing light
To the objects below,
And long shadows that waltzed
On fresh fallen snow.

My eyes traveled with stars
On a course through the sky
And gave me a feeling
That fortune can't buy.

Angels Driving

*I*n a moonlit sky
Dotted with stars,
Angels in heaven
Are out driving cars.

Once in a great while
One will speed off,
While all the others
Sit idling aloft.

When dawn hits their streets,
Off go the lights,
Parking in garages
On dark stormy nights.

Nature's Blanket

*T*he sky released its magic
In the darkness of night,
The purest of the colors,
The whitest of the whites.

The forest stood in silence
Its creatures all tucked in,
Flakes fell to the frozen ground
Where autumn's leaves had been.

A blanket of fresh powder
That sparkled oh so bright,
Lay upon the forest floor
A snowflake comforter tonight.

CHAPTER 3

Trees and Flowers

The Gardener

*H*e arrives with the morning sun
To his garden of pride and joy,
Captivated by his surroundings,
Following dreams from when just a boy.

His day spent among the flowers
Finding reward in work done:
Plants showing great beauty in color
And growing strong in the summer sun.

Only stopping to wipe away
Sweat that has gathered on his brow,
Never too tired nor discouraged,
Fulfills his caretaker's heartfelt vow.

The warmth of the day all but gone,
For the sun has now found the west,
He gathers up his cart of old tools,
Goes home, knowing he's given his best.

*Written for my friend Rae who never tires
of working in his garden.*

Butterfly Dreams

In silent flight
On summer's breeze
Between flowers
And the trees,

Butterfly wings
Dancing mid-air
Bathed in sunlight
Dressed with care.

The children's eyes
With wonder bold
Hoped to catch one
Just to hold.

Beauty stopped by
As we watched you
Sipping nectar
As you flew.

Church Woods

Morning light comes quietly,
Birds sing to a new sun,
The tree buds swell in knowing
That spring has just begun.

A breeze whispers so softly
Through tender boughs of green,
The stately pine and hemlocks
Just wait there to be seen.

Therein winds a tiny brook
On its course between trees,
Always finds the lake nearby
After winter's freeze.

The road once used by carriages
Bends slowly out of sight,
And disappears after dark
Except on starry nights.

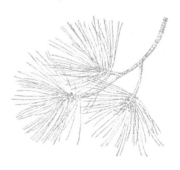

Trilliums

*O*nly by chance I found
Trilliums growing wild,
Picked them for my mother
When I was just a child.

Each year finding their way
From beneath leaves damp and deep,
For months they disappear,
And give beauty time to sleep.

Brushed with a cool spring breeze,
Watered by a heavy dew,
I left them all but one
To be brought back home to you.

Maple Tree

One warm sunny afternoon
Beneath a maple tree,
I listened to a message
On all that life can be.

Family and friends had gathered,
It was a wedding day,
Vows were spoken from the heart,
True love had found its way.

Bride and groom please set your roots
Just like this maple tree,
Growing with the sun and storms,
Be all that you can be.

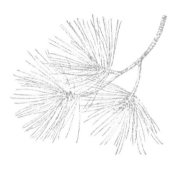

Silence is Golden

A crisp morning air
Awaits me outside,
Along with the hemlocks
And small songbirds that hide.

The trees all silent
While holding the birds,
A sight hard to describe
With ordinary words.

A comforting peace
When the world seems still,
Medicine for the soul
You can't find in a pill.

Silence is golden
The nuggets are small,
I found mine this morning
Wrapped in nature's warm shawl.

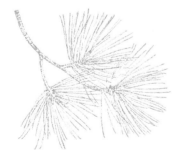

The Flower

*P*laced upon the window sill
Where I could watch you grow,
You brought color to my days
When life was pretty low.

Always there when I woke up,
Nearby when pain was deep,
Standing tall to greet my guests,
And quiet when I'd sleep.

You showed me life was hopeful
Each day I spent with you;
Folks need time to heal and grow
Just as the flowers do.

*This was written while confined
to a hospital bed, where I spent
two months. A friend brought
me an amaryllis and set it on my
windowsill. Watching it grow gave
me hope that I would recover.*

The Rose

*I*n the garden growing
With the other flowers,
Stood a rose by itself
In need of sun and showers.

Petals rolled out softly
To give the color room,
Sending fragrant odors
For as long as it's in bloom.

Knowing that it's fragile,
Its beauty soon will pass,
Each petal letting go
Laid to rest upon the grass.

Silent Message

*B*eside a swift running brook
Under the hemlock trees,
Could feel the touch of autumn
From a cool northern breeze.

The leaves gave a subtle sign
That change was on the way,
The sky was growing darker
I knew I couldn't stay.

If only for a moment,
I'd hear the silence sent,
I understood its message
And kept its hushed intent.

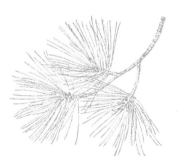

Hillside by
the Lake

$\mathcal{A}$ warm summer sun
Will open the flowers,
They're fed by nature
With dew and rain showers.

Blossoms of clover
Beside white Queen Anne's lace,
Tall-stemmed buttercup
With a bright yellow face.

Dance each passing day
With the lake winds that blow,
All wait in knowing
Their one mission to grow.

All work together
On a hill by the lake,
Offering beauty,
But nothing they take.

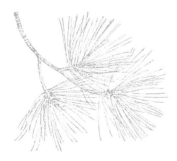

Stone Fence
in the Woods

A fence built of fieldstone
Still winds between the trees,
Placed with care long ago
Stones scattered with autumn leaves,

Through deep snows of winter
And the warm summer's sun,
In a quiet forest
Where the deer and squirrels now run,

Ferns and moss have covered
Stones aged by Father Time,
Past borders and reasons
Now quietly left behind.

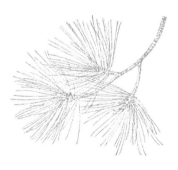

Listening to
the Trees

I came to listen carefully
To what the old trees would say,
Knowing that they had wintered well
And new leaves were on the way.

The morning sun lay on the bark
Trees weathered by the seasons,
Would need to lose a few worn limbs
Wet snow and wind the reasons.

Limbs and leaves will provide cool shade
To shelter the place I'll sit
And listen to the summer winds
Blow songs and secrets through it.

Let nature's peace sweep over you,
As the sun flows into trees,
Drop all your worries from within
Like leaves float on autumn breeze.

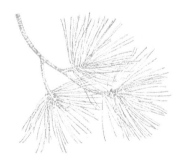

Doe at the
Apple Tree

*S*he came with hesitation
But the temptation proved too great,
Daylight now was nearly gone
And evening darkness wouldn't wait.

The sweetness of the apples
That had fallen from the old tree,
Kept her mostly occupied
Yet, some attention was on me.

Eating her fill in minutes,
Leaving as quiet as she came,
The wildness in her nature
For that moment appeared quite tame.

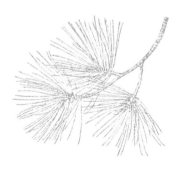

Where the Trees
Meet the Sky

*F*ar from all busyness
That follows us all week,
Sits a rustic cottage
Where peace and quiet meet.

Crackling of a fire
To settle winter's chill,
Bringing warmth to the heart
That comes from sitting still.

Surrounded by forest,
And cool babbling stream,
Stars lighting the skyline,
Sits this place made to dream.

*A friend let me use this beautiful
cabin called "Humpty" for a quiet
weekend to start my work on this
book. Thank you Sally.*

CHAPTER 4

Land and Lake

On the
LaPlatte River

*I*t wasn't a warm sun
On that clear spring day;
It wasn't that the breeze
Had asked me to stay.

'Twas sounds of the water
Stirred by old grey oars,
And new vegetation
Growing on its shores.

The wood ducks and turtles
Playing in the brook
Were my invitation
To ponder and look.

There's no words to describe
All I saw that day,
The welcoming pleasure
To see spring come today.

Lonesome Loon

*S*omewhere in the morning fog
On calm waters of the bay,
There I heard a calling loon
That beckoned me to stay.

Its song seemed to cut the air
And echo from shore to shore;
Its mournful sound touched my heart,
Notes I'd not heard before.

Waiting long beneath those trees
That still held the leaves of fall,
Never did I get to see
The loon that gave that call.

When I left because of time
I carried away this sound:
Echoed songs of a loon
When peace that day was found.

Finding Peace

*S*earching for the quiet,
That's sometimes hard to find,
To put aside my thoughts
And rest my weary mind.

Hidden in the mountains,
Floating on a small lake,
I cast aside all thoughts
And took a needed break.

Within heaven's vast sky
On this clear starlit night,
Peace rose with the full moon
To make the world right.

Wildflowers and tall trees
Come together it seems,
Their beauty reminders
To pause, linger, and dream.

Down by
the Lake

*S*ay – shall we sit
Beneath a shade tree
Down by the lake?
Just two – you and me.

Let's reminisce
Back just a few years,
Sharing old tales
Shedding a few tears.

We can watch boats
Until the sun falls,
Or wait for loons
With tremolo calls.

It's not just sounds
Or beautiful views,
A peace was found
While I sat with you.

Strolling With Eliza
(a brown Swiss beauty)

We walked slowly, side-by-side
Along the wire fence,
Where green and tender blades stood
Of grass that was more dense.

Stopping our leisurely stroll
For her to have a snack,
It was her way of asking
For me to scratch her back.

I looked at her puzzled face;
She looked right back at me.
I pondered, what's she thinking?
What can she really see?

I spoke about the beauty
In views we both could see,
Acknowledged that just for now
We were content to be.

Nothing else seemed important
Walking back to the herd,
Our time together treasured
Though she couldn't speak a word.

Whimsey Meadow

*W*here the wildflowers bloom
And songbirds come to stay,
Butterflies and bumblebees
Stop to rest on their way.

Trails winding through the meadow
Where berry bushes grow,
Through the green grass of summer
Visitors come and go.

As the red sun slowly sets,
Bright stars come into view,
Leaves you with feelings that
This world was made for you.

(Definition of whimsey- fanciful creation)
Whimsey Meadow is located on the
walking trails at Shelburne Farms, just
below Lone Tree Hill.

The Carriage Road

*O*ld sounds of horse and carriage
Once again stirs the air,
Bygone pleasures to savor
Good fortune had us there.

Butterflies in clover fields
And horses know the way,
We trot along as sun sets
Fine end to summer's day.

We passed beside blue waters
Heard bluebirds in the trees,
Felt warm wind kiss our faces
From a southern stirred breeze.

For just a little while
We sensed a presence there
Of those that came before us
In a timeless place still shared.

Earth and
Heaven Meet

*W*hen the sun slowly sets
And bids us good night,
Welcome the arrival
Of the moon's slow flight.

It's a clear sky at night,
All stars hung in place,
Then gone by morning
Not leaving a trace.

Here a fresh fallen snow
Blankets the cold ground,
And clings to tree branches
Without making sounds.

Sweet notes of mourning doves
Serenading dawn,
The birds build their rough nests
In trees on the lawn.

Here bees and butterflies
Share warm summer breeze,
And chipmunks and squirrels
Scamper through the trees.

These green forests and fields
Where wildflowers grow,
Greeting the new seasons
With nature's great show.

One Leaf
on a Journey

*L*eaves hang on a branch
Where the seasons aren't long,
And patiently wait
Near the chickadee's song.

Fall touched its small veins,
The leaf had to let go,
It gently dropped down
To the brook just below.

Set gently adrift
In a clear mountain stream,
Where hikers stop by
For a moment to dream.

Over rough rapids
And strong whirlpools that hold
One leaf, one journey,
Now in waters run cold.

Somewhere in silence,
Where the calm waters wait,
Surrendering leaf
Has now come to meet fate.

The Kiss
on Mirror Lake

Our two hearts close together
Held on a page in time,
A gentle kiss was given
Beneath the warm sunshine.

On a quiet mountain lake
We sat for a just awhile,
Talked about God's many gifts
In Adirondack style.

Our tiny rowboat weathered,
The oars a little worn,
One life jacket between us
From which the straps were torn.

We shared that special moment,
Forever in my mind,
My wife, my friend, my partner,
My true love, so kind.

Dashing Through the Snow

A ringing of sleigh bells
Echoed from the trees,
Cold stung hands and faces
As does an arctic breeze.

The old grey wooden sleigh
Creaked from years of wear,
Pulled by two Percherons,
A stellar, strong pair.

Yet just the simple joy
Dashing through the snow,
Brought warm smiles to faces
Bouncing to and fro.

A mug of hot cider
To shake off the chill,
Mix sleigh bells and snowflakes
For North Country thrills.

A Special Thanks

I would like to offer my thanks to the following people:

To my wife, Candy, for allowing me the time and space to write, and for her endless support and help with my revisions.

To my sons, Jeremy and Travis Bessette, for capturing my favorite places on Shelburne Farms with their cameras and for contributing the wonderful photographs for the book cover and the four chapters.

To the women at Wind Ridge Publishing, for believing in me. I offer my thanks to Holly Johnson, publisher, for giving me the opportunity of a lifetime and for fulfilling a dream; Lin Stone, my editor, for helping me to understand the process of writing a book and teaching me the value of revisions; Margo Callaghan, my graphic designer, for her creativity and generosity, and Laurie Thomas, for many hours of layout and patience with all of my changes.

To my friend, Roz Graham, for writing a biographical introduction on my behalf.

To my neighbor, Amanda Provost, for the time she spent teaching me computer skills and for providing ongoing computer support.

Last but not least, to all of my family and friends for inspiration and encouragement. It is my very good fortune that you are too numerous to mention on just one page.

Thank you, one and all.

Rick Bessette

CPSIA information can be obtained
at www.ICGtesting.com
Printed in the USA
BVOW11s0027170616
452275BV00004BA/8/P